THE EAR
AND HEARING

Revised Edition
Steve Parker

Series Consultant
Dr Alan Maryon-Davis
MB, BChir, MSc, MRCP, FFCM

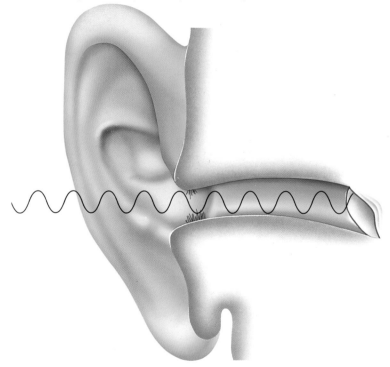

Franklin Watts
London • New York • Toronto • Sydney

Words in bold appear in the glossary

© 1989 Franklin Watts

Original edition first published in 1981
First Paperback Edition 1991
Published in the United States by
Franklin Watts Inc.
95 Madison Avenue
New York, NY 10016

Parker, Steve.
  The ear and hearing.

  (Human body)
  Includes index.
  Summary: Examines the anatomy of the ear, how the ear
receives sounds and transfers them to the brain, how
to protect our hearing, and current developments in
hearing aids and ear surgery.
  I. Title. II. Series: Parker, Steve.   Human body.
QP462.2.P37   1989   612.8′5   88-51611
ISBN 0-531-10712-4 (lib.)/ISBN 0-531-24601-9 (pbk.)

Illustrations: Andrew Aloof, Bob Chapman, Howard Dyke, Hayward Art
Group, David Holmes, Abdul Aziz Khan, David Mallot.

Photographs: Allsport 37; by courtesy of British Aerospace 31; Chris
Fairclough 25; Hutchison 5; Maggie Murray 16, 27t; NHPA 11; Science
Photo Library 9, 12, 15, 21, 34; Vision International front cover; John
Watney 23b, 27b; ZEFA 23t.

Printed in Belgium

Contents

Introduction

Our two ears, sticking out from the sides of our heads, may not appear very delicate or complicated. But these outer ear flaps are only part of the entire ear structure. They work as sound collectors that funnel sound waves into the **ear canal**. This leads to the inner parts of the ear which actually do the "hearing." Tiny, complex and sensitive mechanisms buried within the skull bone, out of sight, are the main hearing organs.

The inner parts of the ear not only hear, they are also involved in balance. They contribute to our "positional sense" by which we know which way is up and which is down. The balance and positional organs enable us to move around confidently without making clumsy movements, or to stand still on one leg without falling over. They also enable us to walk steadily ahead in total darkness, when our position cannot be assessed by the eyes.

Compared with many other animals, our hearing is reasonably sensitive. We can adjust quickly to a great range of loudness – from the roar of a jetliner passing overhead, to the quiet swish of wind in the grass a few seconds later. We can also hear a wide range of sounds **frequencies (pitch),** from the low notes of a tuba or bass guitar to the high squeaks of a piccolo or violin.

Hearing does not involve the ears alone. The ears pick up sound vibrations, turn them into nerve signals, and relay them to the brain. It is in the brain that we interpret and "make sense" of the sounds we hear.

△ Thousands of people gather at an open-air festival. In the middle of the crowd is the engineers' tower. Here, electrical signals from the instruments and voices are mixed and adjusted before being fed into the huge speakers and turned into sounds.

1000 Hz = 1kH

Elephant 20 Hz-10 kHz

Finch 100 Hz-15 kHz

Cat 30 Hz-46 kHz

Dog 20 Hz-30 kHz

Chimp 100 Hz-30 kHz

Man 20 Hz-17 kHz

Whale 40 Hz-80 kHz

Spider 20 Hz-45 kHz

Bat 20 Hz-160 kHz

20   60   200   600   2   6   20   60   200
  40   100   400   1   4   10   40   100

▷ Many animals have a much wider range of hearing than us, as shown in this chart. Elephants can hear very low notes, while bats can hear sounds far too high-pitched for us to detect.

5

The parts of the ear

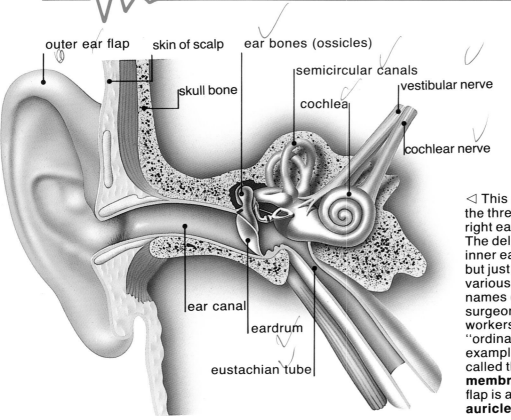

outer ear flap

skin of scalp

ear bones (ossicles)

skull bone

semicircular canals

vestibular nerve

cochlea

cochlear nerve

ear canal

eardrum

eustachian tube

◁ This cutaway view shows the three main parts of the right ear, seen from the front. The delicate organs of the inner ear are almost behind, but just below the eye. The various parts have scientific names (used mainly by surgeons and other medical workers) as well as more "ordinary" names. For example, the eardrum is also called the **tympanic membrane**, and the outer ear flap is also known as the **auricle** or **pinna**.

The ear has three main parts, each with its own special functions. The **outer ear** consists of the ear flap on the side of the head, made of skin and cartilage; the ear canal (the tube leading inward), about 2.5 centimeters (1 in) long in an adult; and the **eardrum**, a thin, tough and flexible membrane at the end of the canal.

The **middle ear** lies beyond the eardrum. It is an air-filled cavity about 15 millimeters (0.6 in) deep, the same from front to back, and some 5 millimeters (0.2 in) wide. Inside are three tiny bones, the smallest bones in the human body.

These bones are called ear **ossicles**. A small tube, the **eustachian tube**, leads forward and inward from the middle ear cavity to open into the back of the throat. It is about 40 millimeters (1.6 in) long.

The **inner ear**, the most complex part, contains the sense organs for hearing and balance. These delicate, fluid-filled structures fit snugly into a series of hollows and tubes, called the **bony labyrinth**, in the bone of the skull. The organs are the **cochlea**, the three **semicircular canals**, and two sacs – the **utricle** and **saccule**. Together, these organs are called the **membranous labyrinth**. That is because their walls are made of thin membranes, and because they twist and turn to form a miniature maze of tubes, canals and bulges lying within the thickness of the skull bone.

The part of the inner ear concerned with hearing is called the cochlea. It is a snail-shaped spiral tube about 3-4 centimeters (1.5 in) long that winds around about $2\frac{3}{4}$ turns. Within this tube, the great variety of sounds are turned into nerve signals.

Near the cochlea are three looped tubes called the semicircular canals. The fluid in these canals responds to movements of the head, in any direction. At the base of each canal is a small bulge called the **ampulla**: this contains sensory devices that convert the fluid movements into nerve signals.

Where the three canals join, there is a large cavity known as the utricle. Next to this is another slightly smaller cavity, the saccule. These cavities are also filled with fluid and they register the position of the head and which way it faces.

The **cochlear nerve** leads from the cochlea toward the brain. It joins with the **vestibular nerve** from the ampullae, utricle and saccule. This combined nerve then travels a short distance through the skull bone and into the brain itself.

What is sound?

▽ The vibrations of a tuning fork are too small and fast for the eye to see. Dipping the fork in water slows down the vibrations and makes them churn up the water, so that we can see their effect. As the prongs of the fork vibrate in air, they alternately compress and stretch the air next to them. These movements are passed along like a wave in the air, although they gradually fade with distance. The greater the wave's amplitude, the louder the sound.

Sound is a form of energy, like light and heat, but unlike them, sound travels quite slowly. If there is a thunderstorm some distance away, the light from the lightning flash reaches your eyes in a fraction of a second. The crash of thunder is generated at the same time, but it may take several seconds to travel the same distance to your ears. At sea level, sound travels through air at about 1,220 km per hour (760 mph). This is the "speed of sound."

Sound is simply vibrating molecules. When a sound is produced, it causes the tiny molecules in air (or any other material) to vibrate, or shake to and fro. This starts the next group of molecules vibrating, which in turn starts the next group – and so the sound travels outward from its source.

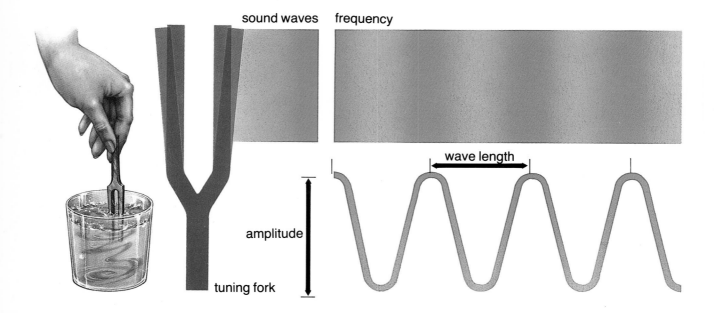

sound waves   frequency

wave length

amplitude

tuning fork

We can imagine sound traveling as waves, like the waves in a wind-blown field of grass. As the vibrating prong of a tuning fork moves one way, it presses on the air next to it. Then it moves back the other way and rarifies or "stretches" the air. These very fast alterations of pressure can be represented as a wave-like series of peaks and troughs in a graph of air pressure. The height, or **amplitude**, of the peaks and troughs indicates the loudness of the sound (page 10).

The distance between one peak and the next (or one trough and the next) is the **wavelength.** This is related to the frequency, the number of to-and-fro vibrations made by the molecules in one second. The longer the wavelength, the fewer vibrations there are in each second, because the molecules have farther to travel, and the lower the frequency. A short-wavelength, high-frequency sound is heard as a high-pitched note, like a flute. A long-wavelength, low-frequency sound is heard as a low-pitched note, such as a bass drum.

▽ The television studio has controls for sound as well as pictures. The black console on the lower right is the sound mixer. It bears "faders" – white sliding knobs that adjust the levels of various parts of the soundtrack. The central keyboard controls the various tape-editing machines.

Loudness and softness

Even in the middle of the night, in the quiet of the country, it is rarely completely silent. Even if we cannot hear any sounds at all, it does not mean there are none.

Some sounds are too quiet for us to hear. The loudness or volume of a sound is measured in **decibels** (dB). The softest whisper measures some 10 to 15 decibels, which is the quietest sound we can detect. Some animals such as dogs have more sensitive ears than us, and they can hear even quieter sounds.

We may not hear other sounds because they are outside the range of frequencies that we can detect. The frequency of a note is measured in hertz (Hz), one hertz being one cycle of vibrations per second (page 8).

The lowest notes that the human ear can pick up have a frequency of about 15 to 20 hertz, and sound like a low rumble. The highest notes that we can detect are around 15,000 to 20,000 hertz. Our ears become less sensitive with age, so that elderly people often cannot hear above 12,000 hertz.

A dog's ears pick up sounds higher than 30,000 hertz. This means it can hear the high-pitched squeaks of a bat, which uses sound as "radar" to find its way through the darkness. A dog whistle is silent to us because it produces very shrill, high-frequency sounds which our ears cannot detect, but a dog's ears can. Some creatures, such as porpoises and moths, can hear sounds of 100,000 hertz and beyond.

Sounds deafening!

Loud noises can damage the ears and cause a form of deafness, especially if we are exposed to them for any length of time.

- A ticking watch measures 10-20 decibels.
- A babbling brook measures 30-50 decibels.
- Normal talking registers 60-70 decibels.
- Loud music that is difficult to "talk over" is 85-90 decibels.
- A pneumatic drill at one meter (3.2 ft) away, or a nearby jet engine, measures 120–140 decibels.
- Sounds above about 90 decibels can damage hearing. The risk of damage increases with length of exposure.
- Some people in charge limit the volume of sound at events such as discos and rock concerts, to protect the ears of the audience.

▷ A greater horseshoe bat, captured by the photographer's sudden flash, homes in on a moth in the darkness. It is guided by its "radar" – echoes of the high-pitched squeaks it utters as it flies. These bounce off the moth and back to the bat's ears.

Sound waves enter the ear

The outer ear collects **sound waves** and guides them into the ear canal. The waves are funneled along the canal and bounce off the eardrum at the end, causing it to vibrate.

Our ear flaps may not look like very efficient "sound funnels." Indeed, they are not particularly effective compared to those of some animals. Rabbits, horses and many other creatures, have large, movable ears that can pinpoint the source of a sound. The ear actually rotates to detect the direction from which the sound waves are loudest. These animals can also assess the direction of a

△ An ear dilator, which holds open the ear canal to allow sounds to reach the eardrum.

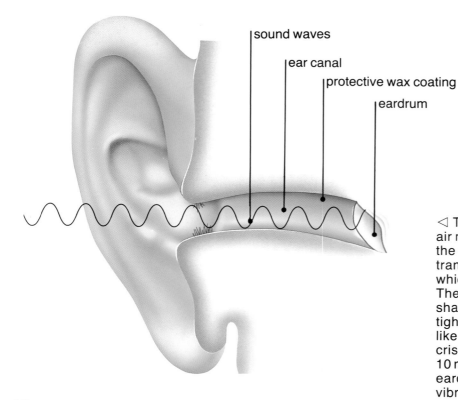

sound waves

ear canal

protective wax coating

eardrum

◁ The energy in the vibrating air molecules passes along the ear canal and is transferred to the eardrum, which vibrates "in sympathy." The eardrum is a thin, heart-shaped membrane stretched tightly across the ear canal like a drumskin. It is made of criss-crossed fibers, about 10 mm (0.4 in) across. The eardrum, in turn, passes the vibrations to the middle ear.

labels: eagle, elephant, fennec fox, frog

sound source by gauging the tiny difference between the time sound waves that come from the side strike one ear before traveling onward the short distance to strike the other ear.

We can do the same, although less precisely. If we hear a noise, we can turn our heads to "face the sound" at which point the sound waves reach both ears at the same time. We can pinpoint a sound source to within two or three degrees, which involves detecting a time difference of less than one ten-thousandth of a second.

The ear canal is about 25 millimeters (1 in) long and slightly S-shaped. It is lined with thin skin covered with very fine hairs. In the skin are tiny glands, which make sticky ear wax or **cerumen**. The wax helps to trap dust and dirt particles. As we talk and eat, jaw movements encourage the wax to move along and out of the canal, keeping the canal clean.

△ Ears vary in size and shape in the animal world. Large ears, like those belonging to the elephant and fennec fox, can pick up very faint sounds. They also act as "radiators" to help rid the owner of excess body warmth in very hot weather. A bird's ears are hidden under its feathers. A frog's ears can be seen as large skin-like disks behind the eyes.

13

The amplifying ear

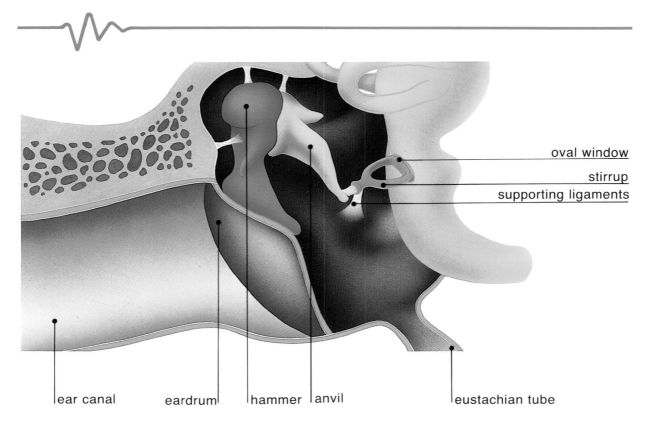

oval window
stirrup
supporting ligaments

ear canal   eardrum   hammer   anvil   eustachian tube

The outer ear changes the form of the sound waves, converting the energy of the vibrating air molecules into vibrations in a solid substance – the skin of the eardrum. The middle ear amplifies these vibrations (makes them more forceful) and passes them on to the delicate sense organs of the inner ear.

Inside the middle ear cavity are the three tiny ear bones, or ear ossicles. They are called the hammer, anvil and stirrup, from their shapes. (Their scientific names are **malleus, incus** and **stapes**.)

The largest ear bone is the hammer. Its "handle" is attached to the eardrum, making a ridge that can be seen on the outer side of the eardrum. The next bone in the chain is the anvil, which connects to the

△ The three ear bones (here colored for clarity) are held in position in the middle ear cavity by miniature ligaments. The eustachian tube allows the air pressure in the middle ear to be equalized with the air pressure in the throat – which is the same as the outside air pressure. In this way, changes in atmospheric pressure can be transferred to the middle ear cavity. Otherwise such changes might make the eardrum bulge, reducing its ability to vibrate freely.

◁ The three ear bones as seen under the scanning electron microscope. The hammer is at the top, the anvil in the middle, and the stirrup at the bottom. Like other bones, they each contain holes for blood vessels and nerves.

third bone, the stirrup. At the far end, the stirrup is attached to another "drum" – the **oval window**, set into the lining of the inner ear.

The three ear bones are hinged together by miniature joints, just as the large leg bones hinge at the knee joint. Together, they act like a series of levers. Vibrations pass from the eardrum through each bone in turn and become more intense as they do so, owing to the leverage effect. If the sounds become too loud, a small muscle contracts to dampen the vibrations of the bones. This helps to protect both the bones and the delicate inner ear from damage.

Amplifying soundwaves

The different parts of the outer and middle ear act together to amplify vibrations, permitting the organ of hearing (cochlea) to function more effectively.
- The outer ear flap and ear canal funnel sound waves onto the eardrum, doubling their intensity.
- The eardrum is about 20 to 30 times the area of the oval window.
- In addition, the lever effect of the three ossicles doubles the intensity of vibrations passing along them.
- The overall effect is that the force of the vibrations increases some 20 to 30-fold by the time they reach the inner ear.

15

The cochlea

△ The tympanometer is a device for testing how well the eardrum and middle-ear bones are working. The machine is small enough to be carried in a briefcase.

The snail-shaped cochlea, in the inner ear, is the main organ of hearing. It converts the energy of vibrations into electrical nerve impulses, which are sent along the cochlear nerve to the brain.

It is easier to understand the structure of the cochlea if you imagine it uncoiled and straightened out. It would then form a tapering tube, about 30 millimeters (1 in) long and 3 millimeters (0.12 in) across at the wide end.

Running through the length of the cochlea are three compartments, like three tubes that have been squashed together to flatten their sides. The membrane-covered oval window is set in the upper compartment, the scala vestibuli, at its bulbous base. The lower compartment is known as the scala tympani. It also has a membrane-covered "window" in it, the **round window**, which is much smaller than the oval window.

Both of these compartments are filled with a liquid called **perilymph**. At the tip of the cochlea, the two compartments are joined by a tiny gap through which perilymph can flow. The much smaller central compartment is called the cochlear duct, or scala media. It has flexible, membranous walls and is filled with a liquid called **endolymph**.

As the stirrup bone rocks to and fro against the oval window, it sets up vibrations in the liquid on the other side. These vibrations are transmitted through the perilymph, and set up vibrations in the walls of the cochlear duct. This contains special cells that turn vibrations into nerve messages.

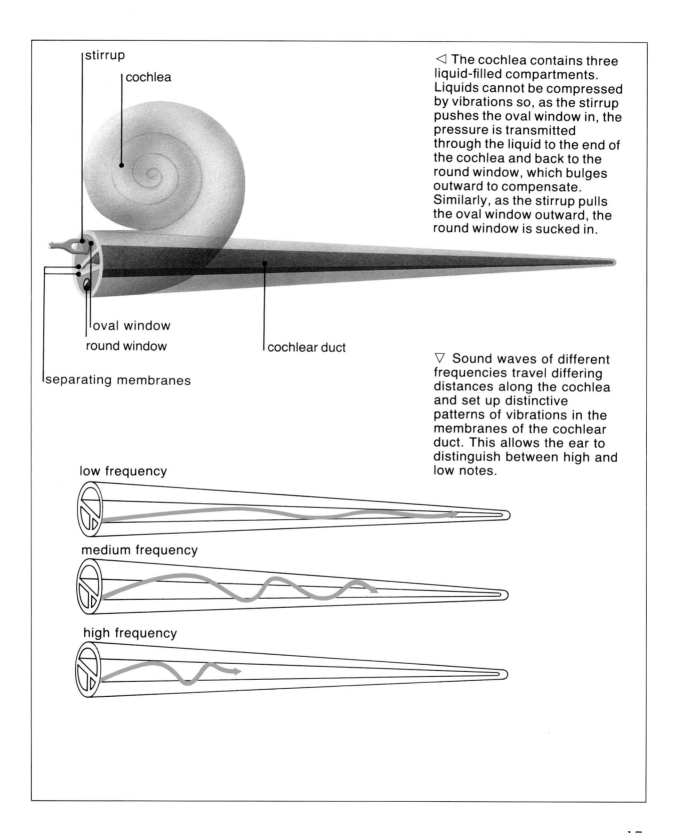

stirrup

cochlea

◁ The cochlea contains three liquid-filled compartments. Liquids cannot be compressed by vibrations so, as the stirrup pushes the oval window in, the pressure is transmitted through the liquid to the end of the cochlea and back to the round window, which bulges outward to compensate. Similarly, as the stirrup pulls the oval window outward, the round window is sucked in.

oval window

round window

cochlear duct

separating membranes

▽ Sound waves of different frequencies travel differing distances along the cochlea and set up distinctive patterns of vibrations in the membranes of the cochlear duct. This allows the ear to distinguish between high and low notes.

low frequency

medium frequency

high frequency

Receiving sounds

The **organ of Corti** forms a long "ribbon" along the lower wall of the cochlear duct. This fascinating and complex structure has three main parts. One is the **basilar membrane**, which forms a strip of the floor of the cochlear duct. Resting on the basilar membrane are sensory cells with hairs projecting from their upper ends. The tips of the hairs are embedded in another thin membrane on top of them, the roof, or **tectorial membrane**, which sticks out from the side wall of the cochlear duct. Nerve fibers run from the sense cells and are gathered together to form the cochlear nerve.

▽ This cross-section through the cochlea shows the central cochlear duct and the organ of Corti that forms part of its "floor."

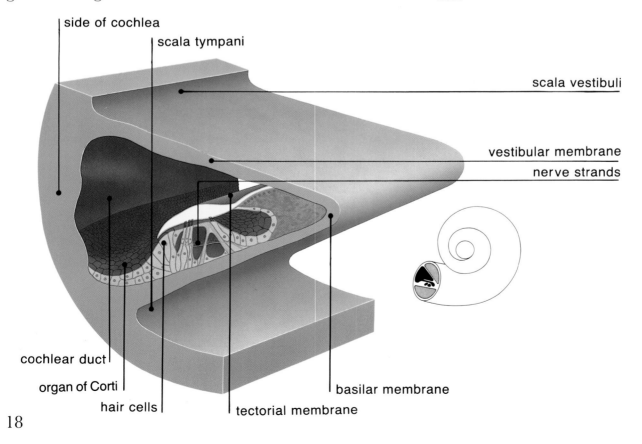

side of cochlea

scala tympani

scala vestibuli

vestibular membrane

nerve strands

cochlear duct

organ of Corti

hair cells

tectorial membrane

basilar membrane

Vibrations in the perilymph and endolymph liquids of the inner ear shake the membranous walls of the cochlear duct. As the vibrations pass through the organ of Corti, they move the basilar membrane in relation to the tectorial membrane, so that one slides past the other. This bends and stretches the hairs of the sensory hair cells, which stimulates them to produce nerve signals.

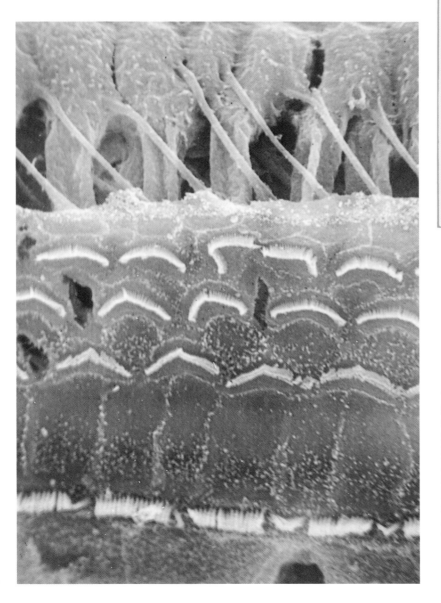

◁ A scanning electron microscope reveals the amazing beauty of the hair cells in the organ of Corti. Here, the tectorial membrane has been removed to obtain a view looking down on the hair cells. The hairs of each cell in the inner row (below) are in a straight line. In the three outer rows, the hairs of each cell are arranged in a V shape. The "scaffold poles" at the top right are supporting cells.

Nerve signals

Every second, thousands of tiny electrical nerve signals leave the organ of Corti and pass along the cochlear nerve to the brain. The signals carried along the nerve fibers are very simple; it is their pattern that is important. Each sensory hair cell produces a continuous stream of signals. When its hairs are bent in response to vibrations in the cochlear liquid, it sends signals more rapidly. As a result, bursts of extra nerve signals are sent from the organ of Corti to the brain whenever sounds are received.

There are more than 20,000 sensory hair cells in each ear, and each one can "fire" up to 20,000 nerve signals per second – a total of 400 million

▽ Sensors on the ears and head pick up the faint electrical signals that travel along the cochlear nerve to the brain. The resulting chart (left) helps doctors to identify hearing problems.

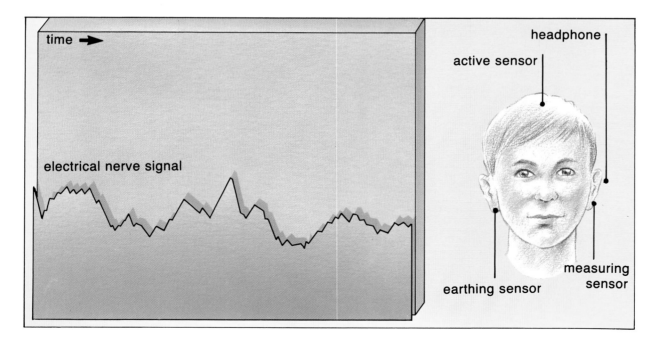

time ➡

electrical nerve signal

headphone

active sensor

measuring sensor

earthing sensor

signals each second. However, the combined cochlear nerve and vestibular nerve (which carries signals from the organs of balance) consist of only about 30,000 nerve fibers altogether. Furthermore each fiber can carry only 1,000 signals each second – a total of only 30 million. Because of this, many signals from the hair cells are lost or filtered out. The problem is partly overcome by passing signals along different nerve fibers in turn, so that more can reach the brain within a given time.

When they reach the brain, some signals "cross over" – that is, those from the right ear cross to the left side of the brain, and vice versa. This probably allows sounds received from each ear to be compared, so that we can decide from which direction the sound is coming.

Sounds are basically energy in the form of vibrations in the air. These vibrations can also pass through solids and liquids, including those that make up the parts of the body. In the past people used to put an ear to the ground to detect the hoofbeats of an approaching horse, since the vibrations traveled much faster through the ground than through the air. In the same way, as we talk the vibrations pass from the throat, mouth and nose through the skull bones to the inner ear, where they stimulate the hair cells of the cochlea. Similarly, as the intestines and other internal organs squirm around, and as the bones and muscles slide and creak against each other, they too transmit vibrations through the body to the inner ear.

This "background noise" is largely filtered out during the process of hearing, partly by damping down the ear-bone movements, and partly, it is thought, by electrical filtering in the brain. This "internal sound" stops it interfering with the more meaningful sounds coming in from outside the body.

▽ This is the "sound shape" of the word "baby," as created by a computer controlled speech synthesizer. After the ear hears this word, the electrical signals passing from ear to brain may follow a similar kind of pattern.

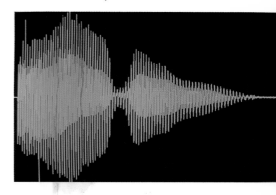

"Sound memories"

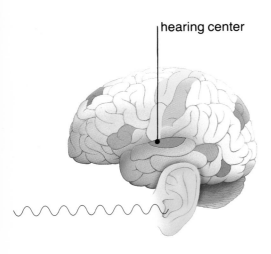

△ Certain areas of the brain's surface, called centers, deal with incoming and outgoing signals from specific parts of the body. The hearing center is shown in red, just above the ear. Among the other centers shown are those for vision (blue), speech (orange) and sound memories (light brown).

Every second, the brain receives millions of nerve signals from sense organs all over the body. How does it deal with such a mass of information?

The surface of the brain, the **cortex**, looks much the same all over, but research has shown that certain parts of it deal mainly with signals from a particular sense, such as sight or touch. These specialized parts are called "centers." The two hearing centers are on the sides of the brain, just above the level of the ears themselves.

It is still not clear exactly how the brain recognizes and understands the signals it receives from the ears, and how the mind "hears." Somehow, patterns of incoming signals are compared with patterns already there, in the form of "sound memories" which are concentrated in a nearby center. The process is extremely complicated, but it is very sensitive.

Sound memories start to build up even before birth. A baby in the womb can hear the sounds of its mother's body, such as her heart beating, as well as louder, deeper noises from outside. Immediately after birth, almost any sound is new and unfamiliar. Gradually we come to link sounds with events; we connect speech with a moving mouth, and a crackling sound with fire.

When a sound is perceived, it is sorted out and compared with sounds in the memory. The brain then decides whether any action is necessary, and if the sound is important enough to remember or if it can be safely ignored.

22

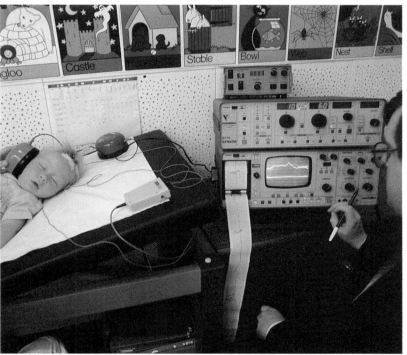

△ Stereo headphones allow us to listen carefully to music, uninterrupted by the usual background noise of traffic or people talking.

◁ A sensitive machine can pick up the tiny electrical nerve messages which pass to the brain, when this sleeping baby's ears hear a sound. The sounds played, and the messages detected by electrodes on the skin, are displayed on the monitor screen and paper chart.

23

Sorting out sounds

The basic process of recognizing and understanding sounds in the brain is poorly understood. Even more baffling are the various ways in which the brain can act as a filter and monitor, without our being aware of it. It is thought that the flood of sounds entering the ear are filtered, clarified and simplified at various points in the brain.

We are hardly ever in perfectly quiet surroundings. There is nearly always background noise of some kind, such as music, traffic or people speaking. If we wish to concentrate on a particular sound, such as one person talking, the brain separates and filters out the many other sounds picked up by the ear. It can do this even when the

▽ Sound waves travel outward from their source. Depending on our position, they reach one ear slightly before the other. We can detect the time difference and so estimate which direction the sound is coming from.

X+1/100000 sec

X

background noise is louder than the sound of the voice – for example, when listening to the whisper of a friend in a crowded classroom.

Another amazing feature of the brain's hearing abilities is called the "cocktail party phenomenon." Imagine you are at a party where several people are having conversations. You are talking to a friend when suddenly, from across the room, you hear your name mentioned by someone else. Yet you were paying attention to your friend and not listening to the other conversation – or were you?

It seems that part of the brain is always listening to sounds and monitoring them, without our being aware of it. As soon as this "monitoring system" detects something of interest, it "pushes" the sound into our consciousness so that our attention is drawn to it. Microphones have been made that are more sensitive than the human ear, but no machine can approach the brain's ability to monitor and untangle sounds.

The same monitoring system operates even when we are asleep. A mother may sleep through the noise of jet planes passing overhead or the wind rattling the windows. But as soon as her baby cries out, even if it is in another room and the cries are faint, her brain recognizes the sound as important and she wakes up.

Human speech presents the ear with many problems, because certain words sound alike or almost alike. Sometimes we cannot distinguish between similar words, but we can identify them because of the way in which they are used – their "context." For example, we might confuse the words "goat" and "coat' if heard on their own. But in the context of a sentence, confusion is much less likely. We would suspect an error if we heard someone say: "It's cold outside, I think I'll put a goat on."

△ A mother may sleep through loud noises, but the cry of her baby wakes her at once. Part of the brain is monitoring incoming sounds even while we sleep, and selecting ones that are important.

Loss of hearing

Hearing relies on a chain of events, from sound waves entering the ear canal to the nerve signals being perceived in the brain. A problem at any stage in the chain can lead to loss of hearing. The word "deafness" is sometimes used to describe this condition, although terms such as "hearing loss" or "hearing difficulty" are common today. In general, someone with normal hearing can detect sounds as quiet as 10 or 15 decibels. Hearing loss becomes a significant problem when a person cannot hear sounds much below 70–80 decibels, the loudest sounds produced in normal speech.

There are two basic types of hearing loss. One is conductive, the other is perceptive (or sensorineural).

In **conductive hearing loss**, the vibrations that represent sound waves do not reach the inner ear. Some causes of conductive deafness are easy to correct. A small object or an accumulation of ear wax may block the ear canal and prevent most of the sound waves from reaching the eardrum. This can be cured by careful syringing of the ear, using a jet of warm water to flush out the blockage.

In some cases the ear canal becomes infected with germs and swollen, a condition known as **otitis externa**. Temporary hearing loss, along with earache, is sometimes caused by an infection of the middle ear cavity (**otitis media**). The middle ear becomes inflamed and pus collects around the eardrum and small bones, stopping them vibrating freely. Usually, when infections such as otitis

Ear diseases
- Tinnitus is a humming, or whistling sound or some other noise in the ear, when there is no such sound reaching it. It is a symptom of several ear diseases.
- Each year, about one person in 100 visits the doctor because of an infection of the ear canal.
- At least half of all children suffer from an infection of the middle ear at some stage.
- Otosclerosis develops in about one person in 250, usually between the ages of 20 and 40 years.
- **Meniere's disease** and **labyrinthitis** are inner-ear diseases that affect the sufferer's sense of balance (page 36).

▷ Children who are hard of hearing can use a microphone to pick up the voice, which is amplified and played back loudly through the headphones. In this way they learn the throat and mouth movements needed for clear speech. They can then remember these movements, even if they cannot hear themselves clearly when the headphones are removed.

externa and otitis media are cured (either naturally or with antibiotic drugs), normal hearing is restored.

Another cause of conductive hearing loss is otosclerosis. Extra honeycombed pieces of bone grow around the stirrup bone, "cementing" it in place so that it cannot pass vibrations to the inner ear. Otosclerosis can be cured by a delicate operation to free the stirrup bone or remove it completely and replace it with a tiny artificial substitute. Mild cases can be helped by using a hearing aid to make the sounds louder.

In **perceptive hearing loss**, there is a fault in the cochlea or the nerve to the brain. If the problem is in the organ of Corti, a hearing aid can sometimes help. However, the hair cells and nerve fibers, once damaged, cannot regenerate: if there is nerve damage, the hearing loss is usually permanent. That is why it is so important to take care of our ears by avoiding very loud noises, especially if the noise is prolonged.

△ Hearing aids detect sound waves coming into the ear, turn them into electrical signals, amplify these and change them back into sounds, which are played towards the eardrum. This aid will fit behind the ear, out of sight.

The importance of sound

Sound is important to everyday life. A large part of learning involves listening to the speech of others, and many recreations, such as music and theater are based on sound.

A person born with severely limited hearing has great problems in learning to talk. It is very difficult to learn to speak when you cannot hear the speech of others – and when you cannot hear your own voice. Children with such hearing loss learn to feel the vibrations of sound, for example by touching the throat of the teacher. Then, touching their own throats, they attempt to make sounds that mimic these vibrations.

▽ In sound recording, a microphone turns sound waves into electrical signals. These can be "coded" in various forms, as shown here. An amplifier makes the signals bigger so that they can drive a loudspeaker and be turned back into sound waves.

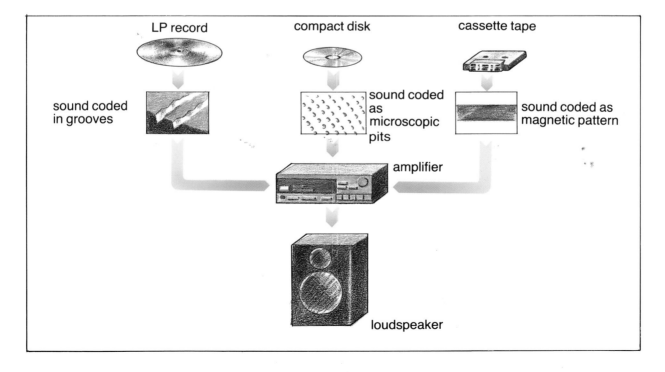

LP record

compact disk

cassette tape

sound coded in grooves

sound coded as microscopic pits

sound coded as magnetic pattern

amplifier

loudspeaker

▽ There are various systems of "talking with the hands." This is one of the finger spelling methods, where individual letters are indicated by position of the hands and fingers.

Standing and walking

The human body, standing on two legs, is not a particularly stable design. It is easy to catch people "off balance" and push them so that they almost topple over. A four-legged animal, with a leg at each corner, is much more stable. This is partly why our sense of balance is so important in everyday life. Without it, we could not even stand still, let alone walk about or bend over.

The sense of balance, or **equilibrium**, is based in the inner ear. Two types of sense organs are involved. One detects movements of the head, while

▽ The sense of balance depends on the movement of liquid in the three semicircular canals. They are arranged at right angles to each other, so movement of the head in any direction can be detected.

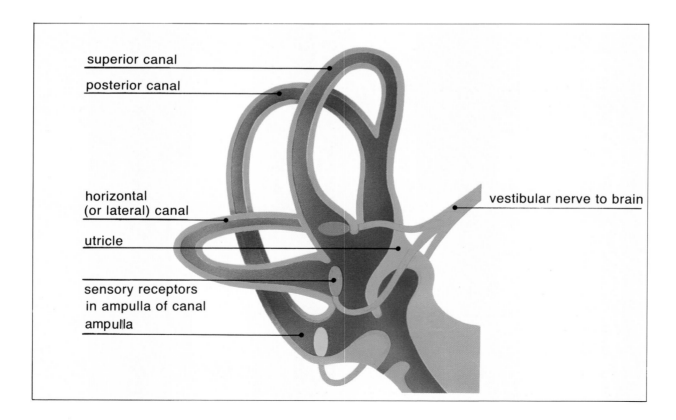

superior canal

posterior canal

horizontal (or lateral) canal

utricle

sensory receptors in ampulla of canal
ampulla

vestibular nerve to brain

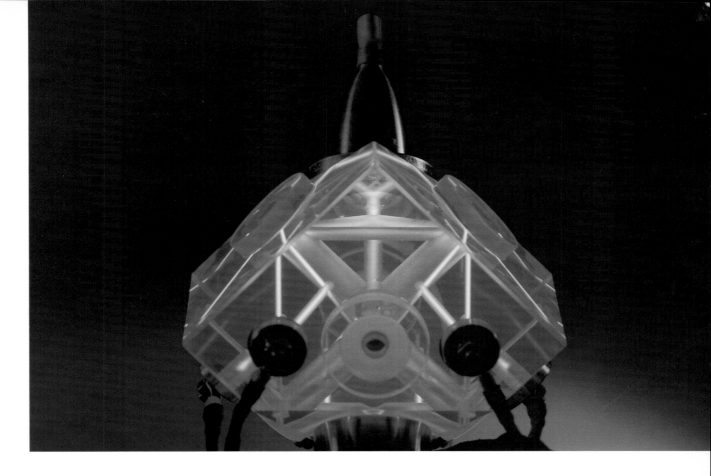

the other "positional" sense detects gravity (page 34).

Three curved tubes, the semicircular canals, detect head movements. Each tube contains two compartments, which are filled with the liquids perilymph and endolymph, like the cochlea. The ends of the tubes are set into the large bulge called the utricle. The canals are 15-20 mm (0.6- 8 in) long.

The positions of the tubes are very important. Any movements can be perceived in terms of three directions, or dimensions: up and down, side to side, and forward and backward. The three semicircular canals are set at right-angles to one another, like the three sides at the corner of a box. The lateral canal is horizontal; the posterior canal is vertical and faces from front to back, while the superior canal is vertical and faces sideways. Each canal detects movement in one of the three dimensions, so between them they can sense movement in any or all of the three dimensions.

△ The "Triad" laser gyro shown above, detects movements in three dimensions, just like the semicircular canals. Laser beams are shone into a cavity inside a block of glass-like substance. As the device rotates, the way the beams cross over changes. Laser sensors detect the changes and feed signals to the control system. Laser gyros are used as sensors to help "balance" aircraft, helicopters, missiles and satellites.

Motion and direction

Turn a glass of liquid quickly. As the glass turns, most of the liquid stays stationary, owing to the phenomenon of inertia. (You can see this more clearly if you sprinkle dark grains, such as pepper, on the surface.) If you keep turning the glass, the liquid eventually begins to turn with it. Then, if you suddenly stop the glass, the liquid carries on spinning for a while before coming to rest.

The liquid in the semicircular canals behaves in a similar way. As the head moves about, the canals move with it, but the endolymph inside tries to remain stationary. Currents are set up as the liquid flows around relative to the walls of the canal. This relative movement of liquid and canals stimulates receptor cells to give the sensation of movement.

At one end of each canal, near the utricle, is a bulge known as the ampulla. In each ampulla is a group of nerve cells called the **crista**, and each cell has a long sensory hair. Over the cells, and surrounding the hairs, is a mass of soft jellylike material called the **cupola**.

As the head turns, the liquid tries to remain stationary. The relative movement causes the cupola to bend, which, in turn, bends the sensory hairs. Like the hair cells in the cochlea, these hair cells react to stimulation by changing the rate at which they "fire" nerve signals. Depending on which canals produce signals, the brain can work out how the head is moving. If you spin around for a time, the liquid "catches up"; when you stop, the liquid continues to spin – and you feel dizzy.

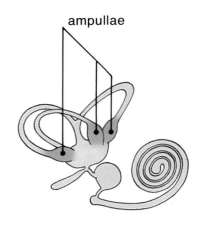

▽ Each of the three ampullae, which contain movement detectors, is sited at one end of a semicircular canal.

ampullae

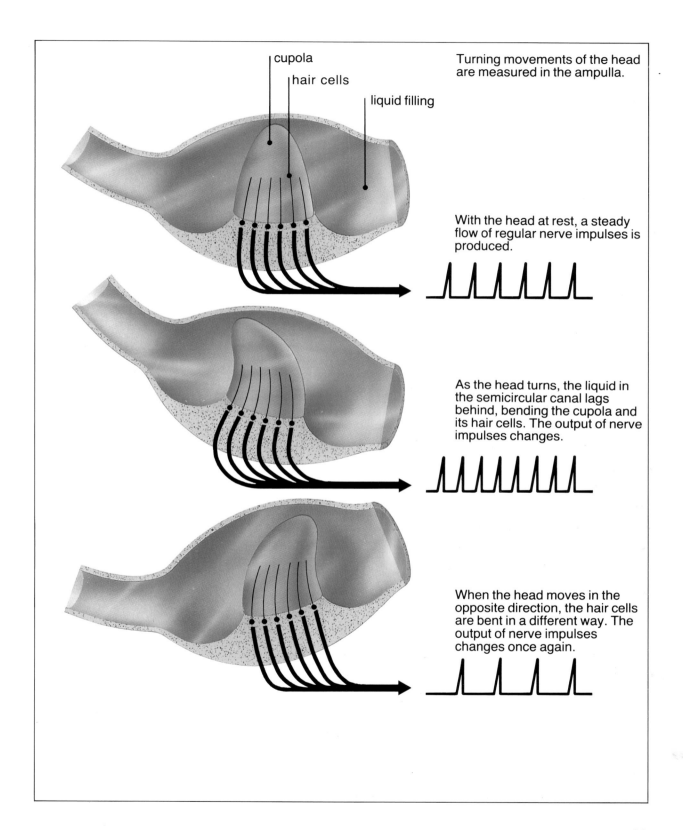

cupola

hair cells

liquid filling

Turning movements of the head are measured in the ampulla.

With the head at rest, a steady flow of regular nerve impulses is produced.

As the head turns, the liquid in the semicircular canal lags behind, bending the cupola and its hair cells. The output of nerve impulses changes.

When the head moves in the opposite direction, the hair cells are bent in a different way. The output of nerve impulses changes once again.

Gravity and movement

The semicircular canals are concerned with detecting movement, or **kinetic balance.** The two bulges of the utricle and saccule are also involved in this sense, but they also measure the head's position when it is still. The saccule and utricle are sometimes called the organs of **static balance**.

The utricle and saccule are filled with fluid, and both contain special sensory areas called maculae in their walls. The maculae are positioned roughly at right-angles to each other, so when one is horizontal, the other vertical.

In each **macula** are banks of sensory hair cells, like the ones in the ampullae of the semicircular canals. The hairs are embedded in a jellylike layer which contains chalky granules known as **otoliths**. Because the granules are relatively heavy, gravity

▽ Who's upside down? Inside the United States' orbiting Space Shuttle, there is no gravity – and so no "up" or "down." In effect, both these astronauts are the right way up.

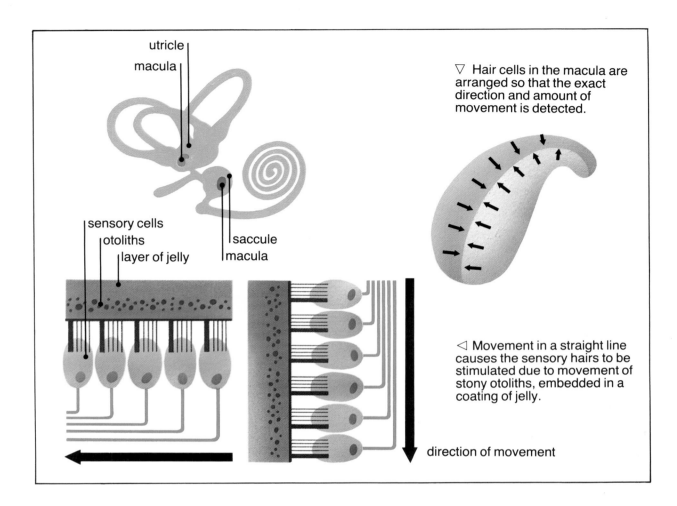

utricle

macula

sensory cells

otoliths

layer of jelly

saccule
macula

▽ Hair cells in the macula are arranged so that the exact direction and amount of movement is detected.

◁ Movement in a straight line causes the sensory hairs to be stimulated due to movement of stony otoliths, embedded in a coating of jelly.

direction of movement

pulls them down, bending the hairs of the sensory cells. Again, this stimulates the cells to change the firing rate of the nerve signals they produce. According to the patterns of signals received from the four maculae (two in each ear), the brain can work out the direction of gravity's pull — so we know which way is "up."

Like the liquid in the canals, the otoliths are subject to inertia. As the head shifts, the otoliths try to remain in their original positions. This also produces changes in the nerve signals sent by their hair cells. It gives the brain information about how quickly the head is accelerating in any particular direction.

A balancing act

Balance is not one single sense; but a combination of several senses. The semicircular canals, utricle and saccule in the inner ear are the main organs. They tell the brain about the position of the head, whether it is moving, in which direction, and whether the movement is speeding up or slowing.

What about the rest of the body? The brain uses information from stretch receptors called proprioceptors, embedded in various muscles, joints and tendons around the body. By analysing the patterns of signals from the proprioceptors, the brain can work out the relative positions of the neck, body and limbs.

Stand up straight, and then bend your head forward at the neck. Despite the information it is receiving from the inner ears, your brain "knows" your whole body has not tilted forward, because the proprioceptors in your neck muscles and joints have reported that your neck has bent, while the rest of your body has remained still.

The eyes are also involved in balance. The brain combines their visual picture of the world with the "gravity and movement picture" from the inner ears. Usually, the eyes confirm what the ears detect. If the inner ears feel that the body is upside down, the eyes will see everything as upside down, too. But in unusual situations, such as in a space vehicle, the ears are fooled by the weightless conditions and the information from the eyes does not fit. This is one reason why astronauts suffer from "space sickness".

Balance in animals

- Many creatures, such as jellyfish and lobsters, have balancing organs called statocysts. Under the influence of gravity and movement, a chalky granule rolls around in a bed of hair-bearing sensory cells.
- An octopus has statocysts and also two sets of three canals at right-angles, like human semicircular canals.
- A fly has two ball-and-stick organs behind its main wings. In flight, these vibrate very fast like tiny pendulums, and act as stabilizers. Their sensory cells also tell the fly about its position, even allowing it to land upside-down on the ceiling.

▷ It looks like a simple dive towards the left. In fact, Veronica Ribot is twisting and turning as she flies through the air. And she has her head down – turn the book around to see that the photograph has been printed upside down! Her combined sense of balance allows her to enter the water safely and smoothly at the end of the dive.

Glossary

Amplitude: the height of a sound wave; associated with the loudness of a sound.

Ampulla: swelling at the base of each semicircular canal, containing sensory cells which detect movement of the fluid within the canals.

Auricle: outer flap of the ear. Also called the pinna.

Basilar membrane: thin sheet of material in the cochlea which vibrates in response to movements in the liquid filling the cochlea. Part of the organ of Corti.

Bony labyrinth: cavity in each side of the skull which contains the inner-ear mechanism. It closely follows the shape of the cochlea and the semicircular canals.

Cerumen: ear wax, produced in the ear canal to lubricate and protect its delicate lining.

Cochlea: coiled tubular structure in which vibrations caused by sound waves are converted into nerve impulses.

Cochlear nerve: nerve that carries signals from the cochlea (the organ of hearing) to the brain.

Conductive hearing loss: hearing loss due to a problem in the vibration-conducting series of structures from earflap to inner ear.

Cortex: surface of the brain in which information received from the ears and other sense organs is processed.

Crista: patches of sensory cells within the ampullae of the semicircular canals. They detect fluid movement.

Cupola: mass of jelly covering the sensory hairs in the ampullae of the semi-circular canals. The jelly shifts as the surrounding fluid moves, bending the hairs and generating a nerve impulse, which is then passed on to the brain.

Decibel: the most common unit used to measure the loudness of a sound.

Ear canal: the short tube conducting sound from the outer ear to the eardrum or tympanic membrane.

Eardrum: thin membrane stretched across the inner opening of the ear canal. Its vibrations are passed to the bones of the inner ear. Also called the tympanic membrane.

Endolymph: liquid filling the central duct of the cochlea. It surrounds the organ of Corti.

Equilibrium: sense of balance that involves movements, detected by the semicircular canals in the inner ear.

Eustachian tube: connects the middle ear with the throat at the back of the mouth. Used to equalize pressure with the atmosphere, protecting the delicate eardrum.

Frequency: the number of vibrations per second of any sound. Frequency controls how deep, or shrill, the sound seems.

Incus: central bone of the three small bones in the middle ear. Takes part in carrying sound from the eardrum to the cochlea. Also called the anvil.

Inner ear: complicated structure inside a cavity in the skull, that contains the sensory organs for hearing, balance and position.

Kenetic balance: balance that involves movements, detected by the semicircular canals in the inner ear.

Labyrinthitis: swelling and inflammation in the membranous labyrinth of the inner ear. It often affects the sense of balance, causing giddiness and a feeling of sickness (nausea).

Macula: area containing sensory cells, within the organs of balance, that measure head position.

Malleus: tiny bone attached to the eardrum, which passes sound vibrations on to the incus. Also called the hammer.

Membranous labyrinth: structure of the inner ear, comprising the cochlea and semicircular canals, extending from the bulky saccule and utricle.

Meniere's disease: an increase in the amount of fluid in the labyrinth of the inner ear, which brings on giddiness and hearing problems.

Middle ear: cavity between the eardrum and cochlea, containing the three ear ossicles (bones).

Organ of Corti: strip of sensory cells resting on the basilar membrane in the cochlea. It receives vibrations in the endolymph, converting them to nerve impulses.

Ossicles: the bones of the middle ear: malleus, incus and stapes.

Otitis externa: soreness and inflammation in the ear canal, usually caused by infection due to germs or a foreign body stuck in the canal.

Otitis media: soreness and inflammation in the middle ear cavity, often accompanied by earache, which is usually caused by germs.

Otoliths: stony particles in the macula of the inner ear, which aid our awareness of gravity and movement.

Outer ear: the external part of the ear (the pinna), the ear canal and the eardrum.

Oval window: membrane-filled "hole" between the middle ear and the bony labyrinth of the inner ear, against which the stirrup bone moves.

Perceptive hearing loss: hearing loss due to a problem in the nerve tissues in the cochlea, cochlear nerve or brain.

Perilymph: watery liquid filling the outer pair of tubes running through the cochlea.

Pinna: the outer visible part of the ear. Also called the auricle.

Pitch: "highness" or "lowness" of a note, due to its frequency. High-pitched sounds, such as from a flute, have a high frequency.

Round window: membrane-filled "hole" between the middle ear and inner ear, which flexes to compensate for pressure changes brought about by the movements of the oval window.

Saccule: area of the inner ear where some of the organs measuring position and gravity are positioned.

Semicircular canals: fluid-filled curved tubes, part of the membranous labyrinth. Movement of fluid through the canals makes us aware of turning sensations as the head is moved.

Sound wave: areas of alternating low and high pressure, which move through air (or any other substance) and, when collected in the ear, are interpreted as sound.

Stapes: one of the three ossicles which passes vibrations into the cochlea

through the oval window. Also called the stirrup.

Static balance: balance when stationary (not moving), involving the utricle and saccule of the inner ear.

Tectorial membrane: long, thin strip of membrane in contact with sensory hairs in the organ of Corti. Sound vibrations move the tectorial membrane and the sensory cells relative to each other, producing nerve impulses.

Tympanic membrane: the eardrum.

Utricle: with the saccule, comprises the areas in which gravity and position are sensed.

Vestibular nerve: nerve carrying signals to the brain from the various organs of balance in the inner ear. It joins with the cochlear nerve.

Wavelength: distance between the peaks of successive sound waves.

Index

PRINTED IN BELGIUM BY

INTERNATIONAL BOOK PRODUCTION